Contents

Any words appearing in the text in bold, **like this**, are explained in the glossary

Lessons learned

Our scientific and technical understanding today means that humans can do amazing things. We can create lush green golf courses on dusty sand through clever **irrigation** networks. We can grow tropical pineapples in snowy Iceland by harnessing **geothermal** energy sources. We can even build whole cities in bone-dry deserts. What does all this do to the environment?

Disasters

Each year hundreds of environmental disasters affect people all around the world. Natural disasters are hard to avoid but the disasters caused by people are often the result of good intentions gone wrong. Some of the most famous environmental disasters are accidents, such as the *Exxon Valdez* oil spill in Alaska, USA in 1989 and the Gulf of Mexico oil spill in 2010, when 11 people died. In both cases, millions of litres of crude oil spilled into the sea, killing birds and marine mammals. The environmental impact will be felt for years to come.

Star-gazing

The word *disaster* came into English from Latin in the 16th century. It means "bad star". This meaning comes from a time when people believed the position of the stars told the future. When the stars were out of line or in a bad position, it was said that a disaster was about to happen.

From fail to win

This book contains 10 examples of those projects where good intentions were outweighed by unforeseen environmental consequences. As we count down from 10 to 1, the failures become more serious and the lessons learned are more useful. Comparing one failure with another is not an exact science, so the order in which the projects are ranked is a matter of opinion.

From wild bees in Brazil and **dredging** in Dubai, to **toxic** toads in Australia and a shrinking sea in Asia, these "failures" will take you all around the world.

From Fail to Win!
Learning from Bad Ideas

THE ENVIRONMENT

Mary Colson

www.raintreepublishers.co.uk
Visit our website to find out more information about Raintree books.

To order:
☎ Phone 0845 6044371
📄 Fax +44 (0) 1865 312263
✉ Email myorders@raintreepublishers.co.uk

Customers from outside the UK please telephone +44 1865 312262

Raintree is an imprint of Capstone Global Library Limited, a company incorporated in England and Wales having its registered office at 7 Pilgrim Street, London, EC4V 6LB – Registered company number: 6695582

Edited by Andrew Farrow and
  Vaarunika Dharmapala
Designed by Richard Parker
Original illustrations © Capstone Global
  Library Ltd 2011
Illustrated by Jeff Edwards
Picture research by Mica Brancic
Originated by Capstone Global Library Ltd
Printed and bound in China by South China
  Printing Company Ltd

ISBN 978 1 406 21768 1 (hardback)
15 14 13 12 11
10 9 8 7 6 5 4 3 2 1

British Library Cataloguing in Publication Data
Colson, Mary.
From fail to win : learning from bad ideas.
The environment.
577.2-dc22

A full catalogue record for this book is available from the British Library.

Acknowledgements
We would like to thank the following for permission to reproduce photographs: Alamy pp. **13** (© Archive Image), **17** (© Amy Mikler), **43** (© Joerg Boethling); Corbis pp. **5** (Science Faction/© Natalie Fobes), **8** (© Keren Su), **14** (© Bettmann), **37** (© Bettmann), **39** (© Bettmann), **48** (© Roger Ressmeyer), **45** (Sygma/© Igor Kostin); Getty Images pp. **10** (© Adam Jones), **12** (Time Life Pictures/Dick Swanson), **15** (AFP/Walter Astrada), **24** (AFP/David Hernandez), **27** (Robert Harding/Tony Waltham), **29** (Fox Photos/Reg Speller), **31** (Picture Post/Raymond Kleboe), **32** (Picture Post/Raymond Kleboe), **33** (Three Lions), **41** (Robert Nickelsbeg); © NASA p. **26** (Earth Observatory/Jesse Allen, using data obtained from the Goddard Level 1 and Atmospheric Archive and Distribution System (LAADS)); Reuters p. **18** (Darrin Zammit Lupi); Rex Features pp. **7** (© NASA), **21** (Sam Tinson), **34** (Everett Collection); Science Photo Library pp. **19** (Gilbert S. Grant), **23** (Kent Wood), **38** (© Shaun Robinson); Yale University p. **11** (© Michael Marsland).

Cover photograph of the remnants of a formerly busy harbour, Aral Sea, Aralsk, Kazakhstan, Central Asia, January 2000, reproduced with permission of Corbis (Sygma/© Paul Howell).

We would like to thank Andrew Solway for his invaluable help in the preparation of this book.

Every effort has been made to contact copyright holders of material reproduced in this book. Any omissions will be rectified in subsequent printings if notice is given to the publisher.

Our environment is precious and fragile and some disasters are easier to put right than others. Lessons have been learned but, as you will see, we haven't learned everything yet.

These workers are cleaning up a beach in Alaska, USA after the *Exxon Valdez* oil spill in 1989.

Constructing coast

"The World's" islands vary in size from 2 to 8 hectares (5 to 20 acres). Houses and hotels will be built on them. Before "The World", Dubai had 72 kilometres (42 miles) of coastline. "The World" has added 232 kilometres (145 miles) of coast, three times the original amount. Sea currents have been disrupted by the vast construction barriers. This in turn has led to an erosion of Dubai's natural beaches.

For most of us, the idea of a tropical paradise involves sandy beaches with palm trees, clear blue waters, coral reefs, and sun. The Persian Gulf state of Dubai already has all of these things. So why is it trying to recreate paradise?

On a stretch of **barren** coastline, a whole new world has been created. "The World" is an artificial **archipelago** of 300 tropical islands in the shape of a world map. It is just one of a series of artificial island mega-projects in Dubai that are so large that they can be seen from space.

"The World" was the **brainchild** of the ruler of Dubai, Sheikh Mohammed bin Rashid Al Maktoum. He wanted to develop his country's tourist industry and make Dubai famous for ambitious building projects.

This map shows you where "The World" is.

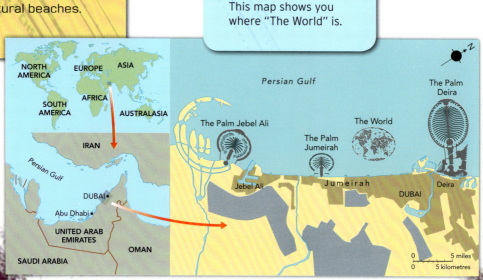

Trouble in paradise

The dream of creating islands is fast turning into an environmental disaster for the Persian Gulf. To construct the islands, massive machines perch on boats to **dredge** the seabed. This involves scraping the rock, digging up the **sediments**, and depositing them elsewhere. The scale of the dredging has clouded the once crystal clear waters with silt. Silt is the mud or clay on the seabed. Once disturbed, it takes a long time to settle down. The clouded water disturbs and can even destroy the delicate **ecosystems** in the water.

Fragile coral reefs, established oyster beds, and important sea grasses are all vulnerable to changes in the water. Marine mammals, such as the rare **dugong** that depend on the grasses and plants on the seabed, have seen their food stock reduced and their numbers are dwindling.

Protecting polders

The Dutch have been reclaiming land for agricultural purposes for centuries. By building barriers around the land and pumping out the water, polders (fields) are created. The barriers, also called dykes, need constant attention to make sure they protect the farmland against flooding. It is Dutch expertise in dredging, engineering, and construction of artificial islands that is being used in Dubai.

This is "The World" development as seen from space in 2009.

The salt problem

All the new hotels and houses on the islands need a fresh water supply. Unfortunately, 70 per cent of Dubai is desert. With monthly rainfall averaging less than 1 centimetre (0.39 inches), all the fresh water in Dubai must be **distilled** from saltwater. This uses vast amounts of energy. Nearly half the world's largest **desalination** plants are dotted along the coasts of Gulf states. When salt is extracted from seawater, it must somehow be disposed of. Most desalination plants pipe this salt back into the sea. In a partly landlocked sea such as the Persian Gulf, the salt doesn't **disperse** quickly and starts to erode marine ecosystems. Fish eggs, plankton, and sea plants are sensitive to even a small increase in the sea's salt content. Any damage to them also affects the creatures who feed on them, such as turtles and dolphins.

The water waste

Dubai is already home to the world's tallest tower and biggest shopping centre, and it will soon boast the world's tallest hotel. From golf courses and fake waterfalls to artificial forests, all these new developments need millions of litres of fresh water.

Golf courses, such as the Creek Golf and Yacht club in Dubai (pictured), use about three million litres of fresh water a day.

FAIL!

"The World" is not enough

In less than 40 years Dubai has transformed itself from a small trading post to an energy-hungry superstate. With unlimited ambition and with little thought for the environmental consequences, there are now plans to create "The Universe". If construction goes ahead, this cluster of islands might finally destroy the very ecosystems that people come to Dubai to see. However much money is spent, and however amazing the technology, building on this scale will have a huge impact on the environment. Clearly there are some lessons still to be learned.

Another desert city

Las Vegas lies in the middle of the Mojave Desert in Nevada, USA. It gets just 10 centimetres (4 inches) of rain per year and the heat in summer dries the land to dust. Yet you can go to Las Vegas and glide in a Venetian **gondola** to your hotel room and watch pirate ships do battle on the sea.

Snow in the desert

In the summer, temperatures in Dubai often rise above 40 °C (104 °F) and water shortages are common. Building one of the world's largest artificial ski resorts in this environment might, therefore, seem unwise. Ski Dubai needs to make a massive 30 tonnes of snow every night to cover its slopes. This requires hundreds of thousands of litres of precious fresh water.

Dubai has one of the highest fresh water uses per person in the world. To keep the snow dome cool enough to stop the snow melting, it is estimated that the energy required is equivalent to 3,500 barrels of oil per day, roughly one barrel (160 litres) per visitor.

Water rationing

As a resort city, Las Vegas is thirsty for energy and water, with swimming pools, spas, gardens, and golf courses to maintain. Most of the city's water is piped in from giant reservoirs, but these are running dry. The city can't escape its desert environment and has had to start water rationing to cope.

What has been learned?

There is a scheme in Las Vegas to encourage hoteliers and residents to get rid of their water-thirsty lawns and convert to xeriscaping instead. *Xeriscaping* is a blend of the Greek word *xeros*, which means "dry", and the word *landscaping*. Under the scheme, only "water smart" desert plants, such as cacti, are planted. It's a small step but it's in the right direction.

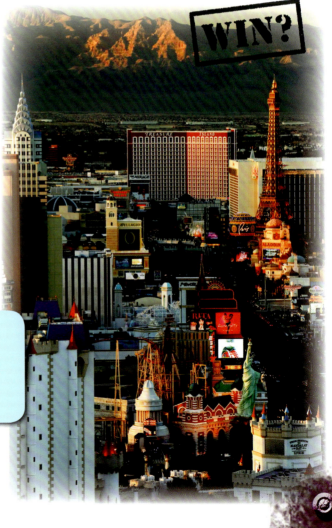

WIN?

The example of xeriscaping in Las Vegas shows that desert cities will need to change if they are to survive in the future.

Agent Orange

Arthur Galston was an American biologist and academic who studied soy bean plants. In the 1940s he discovered that a chemical called triiodobenzoic acid made the beans grow more quickly and plentifully. Galston believed he had made a real breakthrough in the fight against food shortages and hunger. If the chemical was sprayed on to the plants, growing seasons could be longer, **yield** would be higher, and hunger would be avoided.

However, Galston also found that the acid had other, less positive, qualities. If you used too much, all the leaves fell off the plants. This worried him. If that happened to the plant, what would happen to the soil? What impact would the acid have on human health?

While Galston carried on with his research, his early findings were used by scientists in the United States and the United Kingdom. These scientists were developing a range of chemicals, called herbicides, to be sprayed on crops to kill unwanted plants. By the 1950s, these herbicides were used in farming to spray on crops, destroy weeds, and increase yield.

Arthur Galston intended his research to be used for the benefit of humanity.

It wasn't known then, but these herbicides were **toxic**. At this point, our story has to move from US laboratories to the dense forests of Vietnam.

Chemical warfare

Imagine a beautiful tropical forest filled with birds, animals, and plants of every shape and colour. Now imagine a plane flying overhead. You can hear a hissing noise. You don't notice anything at first, but after a few days the leaves start to turn brown and rot off their branches. Birds and animals start to fall down dead. The streams are full of dead fish. What has happened?

In the 1960s and 1970s the United States fought a war in Vietnam, a country of forests, mountains, and jungle. Enemy troops hid in the **impenetrable** forests and US forces needed a way of finding them. The answer came in the form of a herbicide that was known as Agent Orange. It was developed from Galston's original findings about triiodobenzoic acid.

During the Vietnam War, the United States sprayed at least 75 million litres (16.5 million gallons) of Agent Orange on to forests.

The rainbow herbicides

A whole rainbow of chemicals was used by the United States during the war. Agents Purple, Pink, and Green were all sprayed on the forests and fields of Vietnam. All of these chemicals seeped into the ground and the groundwater. They accumulated in the water and became part of the human **food chain**. This is called **bioaccumulation**. When people eat animals and plants contaminated with these chemicals, it can cause them serious health problems.

Galston was horrified at what was happening and campaigned against the use of Agent Orange in Vietnam. He travelled to Vietnam to monitor the impact of the chemical. What he found was disturbing. Nearly 5 million Vietnamese people were exposed to Agent Orange during the war. The chemical caused skin diseases, deformities, and cancers that killed hundreds of thousands of people.

Banning Agent Orange

Arthur Galston was a scientist with a strong social **conscience**. He said, "Science is meant to improve the lot of mankind, not diminish it ... Any discovery ... can be turned either to constructive ends or destructive ends." After a long campaign, it was accepted that pesticides can be very harmful to humans. Agent Orange was finally banned in the United States in 1979.

This soldier is preparing a barrel of herbicide for a helicopter mission during the Vietnam War.

Disease control

In the early 1940s during World War II, two diseases occurring in different parts of the world threatened to kill large numbers of people. Scientists thought that a chemical called dichlorodiphenyltrichloroethane (known as DDT) could be the solution to both of them. DDT is a chemical **insecticide**. It was sprayed over the jungles of the South Pacific to kill malaria-carrying mosquitoes that were infecting and killing soldiers. At the same time, soldiers and civilians in Europe were dusting themselves with DDT powder in the fight against fleas carrying the deadly typhus disease.

What was learned?

It was after World War II that the problems really started. DDT was widely used as an agricultural insecticide to help farmers gain bigger harvests. Not everybody was convinced of DDT's qualities, though. In 1962 the scientist Rachel Carson suggested a link between DDT and cancer, due to bioaccumulation. Carson said that DDT could travel up the food chain through the fatty tissues of animals. Animals who ate other animals would have very high levels of DDT in their bodies. More research was done into DDT's impact on human health. It was found to be a carcinogen, a cause of cancer. In 1972 the United States banned DDT. Many other countries also banned it in the decades to follow.

This truck is spraying DDT in New York, USA, in 1945. Today, it is hard to believe that people once thought this chemical was safe enough to use in public places.

The Nile perch boom

Lake Victoria is the world's third largest freshwater lake. It lies across the borders of Tanzania, Uganda, and Kenya and used to be home to over 500 species of fish. By the end of the 1940s fish stocks were under pressure from over-fishing. More and more people were moving to towns and villages on the lake hoping to make a good living from fishing. Even a small boat could catch enough fish to sustain a family. Some commercial fishing companies operating on the lake were using new, tougher nets and fleets of boats. Fish were being caught quickly and in greater numbers. This meant that there were fewer fish and they were getting younger. They didn't have time to grow up and produce young before they were caught.

The government in Kenya decided to take action. They wanted to protect the fishing industry and the livelihoods of the fishermen. They also wanted to develop the fishing industry as a **cash crop** for the region. A fish called the Nile perch had been successfully introduced to other African lakes, so in the 1950s it was introduced to Lake Victoria.

THE NILE PERCH

Size: 2 metres long (more than 6 feet)

Weight: 200 kilograms (440 pounds)

Appetite: Vast – it will even eat its own species

Predators in Lake Victoria: None

A greedy fish

By the 1980s the Nile perch had "boomed" and established itself as the main fish species in Lake Victoria. Thousands of tonnes of Nile perch were caught.

The small fishing villages couldn't cope with such large catches so warehouses, factories, and fish processing plants were built on the lake's shores. This was great news for the government and the fishermen, but what about the lake?

The introduction of the Nile perch seemed to have been a great success until people realized that the perch had caused a massive imbalance in Lake Victoria's **food chain**. Scientists now estimate that the perch has caused the extinction of around 200 native fish species.

The problem with the Nile perch is that it dominates the lake it is in. It feeds on other fish, shrimps, and insects. Then it goes back for seconds! The perch eats fish that mostly eat algae. Algae are like seaweed and they suck oxygen out of water. As the perch destroys the algae-eating fish, the algae grows more quickly and "chokes" the lake. The oxygen levels in the water drop and fish can suffocate.

Winners and losers

Today the Nile perch is **exported** all over the world and the catch is worth millions of US dollars each year. The big fisheries on the lake benefit from the Nile perch's introduction but the local fishermen who catch other fish have seen their traditional catches get smaller and smaller. There are barely enough native fish left for locals to catch and make a living from.

A matter of taste

Nile perch are so big that they break the traditional nets the local fishermen use (pictured). If the fishermen do manage to catch some, they have to dry the fish over a fire before anyone will buy them at the market. This is because Nile perch are quite fatty and the local people don't like the way they taste.

Hard lives

The shores of Lake Victoria have experienced a building boom to support the Nile perch fishing industry. In 1983 there were an estimated 12,040 boats on the lake. By 2004 there were 51,700, along with 153,000 fishermen.

All along the lakeshore, "boom towns" have been built to house the fishing crews and their families. Without proper planning, these towns lack basic facilities. Only 20 per cent of the towns on the lake have toilets and a mere 4 per cent have electricity. Fewer than 10 per cent of the settlements have a clean water supply.

Life is hard for the people who live in fishing villages like this one on the shores of Lake Victoria. It is particularly hard for children, many of whom are **malnourished**.

What has been learned?

The introduction of the Nile perch into Lake Victoria has been of great economic benefit to Kenya but not to the local villagers. It has also seriously harmed the ecological balance of the lake itself. Introducing non-native species is often positive in the short-term but it is frequently a different story in the long run. Better understanding of the environment and specific **ecosystems** may help us to finally learn from this mistake. Whether the balance of life in and around Lake Victoria can be restored remains to be seen.

The "mile-a-minute vine"

In 1876 at an international show in Philadelphia, USA, a buzz of excitement hovered around the Japanese pavilion. Those who managed to push their way to the front of the crowd could glimpse an attractive eastern Asian plant.

The climbing kudzu vine, with its sweet-smelling purple flowers and large leaves, was an instant hit with American gardeners who planted it to provide shade. It also appealed to farmers in the southern American states where the soil wasn't good enough to grow cereal crops. They planted it to use as food for their animals. No one could have foreseen that the harmless-looking kudzu would soon be known as the "mile-a-minute vine". It has becomeone of North America's most invasive plants.

Better soil, better crops

From the 1930s to the early 1950s the American Soil Conservation Service encouraged farmers in the south-eastern United States to plant kudzu in order to reduce soil erosion and develop the farming industry. By 1935 hundreds of farm labourers had planted over 85 million kudzu seedlings. Farmers were paid nearly $8 an acre as an incentive to plant fields of the vine.

Because of its out-of-control growth in the south-eastern United States, the trailing, coiling kudzu has earned the nickname "the vine that ate the South".

Out of control

People don't call kudzu "the plant that ate the South" for nothing. Unfortunately the south-eastern United States has near-perfect conditions for kudzu to grow totally out of control — hot, humid summers, frequent rainfall, and mild winters. The once-promoted plant has become a pest and has completely taken over.

Climbing killer

Winding up telegraph poles, climbing over houses, and coiling around fences, kudzu is now common throughout most of the south-eastern United States. Kudzu forms a thick blanket of leaves over land, plants, or trees. Light can't get through and so most of the plants underneath eventually die.

Keeping control

Scientists estimate that kudzu is spreading at the rate of 61,000 hectares (150,000 acres) every year. It is spreading more quickly than herbicide spraying can keep up with. The cost to agriculture is around $500 million in lost farmland and harvest. To kill the plant, you have to remove the root crown and all the rooting runners. The crown is like a knot just below the surface, from which all the roots run. Some crowns are pea-sized while others are as big as basketballs. They all then need to be burned to ensure the plant doesn't regrow.

What has been learned?

In 1953 kudzu was named a pest weed by the United States Department of Agriculture. For over 50 years it's been outwitting the authorities but greater controls are now in place for tackling other invasive species. In the United States alone, the fight now includes 25 federal laws, over 40 agencies, an estimated 300 non-federal programmes, 175 organizations, and 140 groups. Maybe the kudzu's days of freedom are numbered.

Biosecurity

Today, most countries are very strict about plants and animals crossing their borders to guard against unwanted invasions of disease. This is called biosecurity and in Australia it is taken very seriously. Fewer than 10 per cent of known pests and diseases exist in Australia and farming is a very valuable industry. When travellers arrive in Australia, they have to throw away anything that might have organic matter in it, such as food or wooden objects. Even shoes are cleaned in case there are seeds lodged in the soles.

People travelling within Australia must throw away food in a bin like this one when they reach a state border.

Killer bees

Everybody makes mistakes, but not many of us can say we have let loose swarms of killer bees across two continents. In 1956 a beekeeper in southern Brazil accidentally released 26 African queen bees. If they had been ordinary bees it would not have mattered. In fact, they were part of a scientific study. Then the poor beekeeper had to go and tell his boss…

His boss was biologist Warwick Kerr. Kerr wanted to breed bees that would be productive in hot climates. Bees are not native to the Americas and were taken there by European settlers in the early 17th century. Bees transport pollen and without this, many plants can't produce fruits, vegetables, and seeds. Over a third of the fruit and vegetables grown in the south-eastern United States are pollinated by bees.

Kerr wanted to increase food production in tropical climates so he took 26 African queen bees to Brazil and planned to breed them with local bees. Unfortunately the bees were released before his studies were completed.

A bad mix

Following the accidental release, the African queens mated with local male European bees. When species mix like this, you get a **hybrid**. The hybrid bee became known as the Africanized honeybee.

Hive take-over, killer bee-style!

Africanized honeybees are cunning. They take over other bee hives by playing it cool and being patient. Usually one or two bees hang around a hive until one of the other bees shares food with them. Once this happens the killer bees are accepted into the hive. It is only a matter of time before large numbers of killer bees enter the hive and take it over. They kill the queen and establish their own queen in her place.

People often call the Africanized honeybee the "killer bee" as it seems to have inherited the worst tendencies from both its parents. It is aggressive and sneaky.

By the early 1960s the bees had attacked farm animals and people who accidentally disturbed their nests. By the 1980s swarms of killer bees had reached as far north as Mexico. The bees spread at a rate of 2 kilometres (1.2 miles) a day or nearly 500 kilometres (310 miles) per year. Today they are common in most of South America, Mexico, Texas, Arizona, and California. Africanized honeybees are considered an invasive species in some American states and are **exterminated**.

The bee on the left is the European dark bee. On the right is the smaller but more aggressive Africanized honeybee.

What has been learned?

We'll never know whether Kerr's studies would have produced a gentler bee. However, he was successful in his aim to breed a bee that could produce lots of honey in hot countries. Brazil, along with Argentina, is now one of the world's biggest exporters of honey. It's an industry worth millions of dollars each year and employs thousands of people.

One small error by an unknown beekeeper many years ago has had many consequences, some good, some bad. From this, and also from studies of human viruses and bacteria, we have learned the importance of biosecurity. This is the protection of the environment and economy from foreign pests and diseases. If nothing is done to control the killer bees, the entire European honeybee population may also become hybridized, with unknown consequences for their behaviour.

Under threat

Africanized honeybees will nest almost anywhere – in the ground, in trees, in buildings, or under bridges. If they think their home or hive is under threat, the bees can become aggressive and have been known to chase people! Hundreds of stinging attacks are reported each year and one or two of these attacks will be fatal.

A nest of Africanized honeybees is destroyed in suburban Mexico City.

The shrinking sea

The Aral Sea was once the fourth largest inland body of water in the world. It was a 66,000 square kilometre (25,500 square mile) expanse of blue. The "sea of islands" was home to many fishing villages that had grown rich on the lake's plentiful fish stocks. Lying on the border between land-locked and water-starved Kazakhstan and Uzbekistan, the sea has been steadily shrinking for 50 years. Why?

In the 1940s Kazakhstan and Uzbekistan were part of the **USSR**. The authorities wanted to create jobs and large-scale industry for the people in the area by building a vast **irrigation** system to grow cotton. This crop could then be **exported**. By 1960 most of the sea's water supply was being diverted to the cotton fields, making the sea shrink.

The two main rivers that feed the Aral Sea are the Amu Darya and the Syr Darya. As the river water was redirected to cotton fields, the rivers' flow into the Aral Sea was reduced to a trickle. As a result, the sea lost 75 per cent of its water and 33,000 square kilometres of seabed is now exposed.

A domino effect

A domino effect is when one thing causes another to happen which then has an impact on something else. The diverting of the waters of the Aral Sea has had a domino effect. It has had unexpected and far-reaching effects.

It's not just the lack of water that has had an impact on the sea. The water that is left is now saltier than before, with nearly three times the original concentration of salt. As a result, more than 20 species of fish have become extinct. Salt granules that lie on the exposed seabed are picked up by the wind and carried away in misty salt clouds. As the wind swirls, the salt acts like a scrubbing brush, scouring all the plants for hundreds of miles around.

North Aral Sea

South Aral Sea (eastern)

South Aral Sea (western)

These rusted ships are stranded on the exposed seabed of the former Aral Sea.

FAIL!

The cotton crops themselves are affected and harvests reduced because the salt kills the plants. Once the plants have gone, there's nothing to hold the soil together. What's left is useless desert. Some farmers have changed from growing cotton to growing rice but rice needs even more water and so millions more gallons are diverted from the sea. So, the domino effect continues.

Bleak outlook

The people who live by the sea have seen their whole way of life change. The once prosperous fishing industry has been virtually destroyed. Former fishing towns along the original shores have become ship graveyards. With no water to irrigate the land and soil that has been eroded by salt, the future looks bleak for the people of the Aral Sea.

What has been learned?

The plight of the Aral Sea is an environmental **catastrophe**. Many people think the destruction of the sea was too high a price to pay for a cotton industry. Today Uzbekistan is one of the world's top cotton exporters but much of the land and the Aral Sea have been ruined in the process.

In the last few years, there have been efforts to save the North Aral Sea. The Kazakhstan government has finally realized the environmental impact of the irrigation network and a dam has been built. Since 2005 the level of the North Aral Sea has risen by a few metres. The salt level has dropped and it is now possible for the local people to fish again. Other governments and environmentalists are working to help save the North Aral Sea. However, the situation for the far larger South Aral Sea seems hopeless.

The example of the Aral Sea shows us that big decisions made for short-term gain can result in long-term catastrophes that are not easily reversed. It also shows us that, in many cases, we are using more water for irrigating farmland than Earth can sustain.

Dead salty

Since 1972 the famously salty Dead Sea, on the border between Israel and Jordan, has lost 20 per cent of its surface area. Like the Aral Sea, it is shrinking. Its water and that of the River Jordan, which feeds it, has been diverted to irrigate farms in the Negev Desert. Unfortunately, salt from the Dead Sea has contaminated the groundwater and many local plant and animal species are now threatened.

The Tanganyika Groundnut Scheme

At the end of World War II, the United Kingdom was still rationing food. Each person was allocated a weekly amount of meat, sugar, butter, and other foodstuffs to make sure there was enough to go around. The war had disrupted the world's economies and there was a global shortage of cooking oil. The British government decided to take action.

In 1945 Tanganyika (now joined with Zanzibar and called Tanzania) in East Africa was under British **colonial rule**. Tanganyika had no real resources or crops to **export**. The British government thought it had found a solution to both its own and Tanganyika's problems.

The Tanganyika Groundnut Scheme was a very bold agricultural experiment. The plan was to cultivate peanuts, also known as groundnuts, in parts of Tanganyika. The peanut crop would thrive in such a hot country. Tanganyika would have a **cash crop** to harvest and the oil from the nuts could then be exported back to the United Kingdom for domestic use. It was a brilliantly simple idea and full of good intentions. Unfortunately a lack of organization, resources, and real understanding of the environment led to a series of failures that would be comical if they weren't so damaging.

Rationing continued after World War II. These people are lining up to collect their ration books in 1951.

A simple plan

The plan was very simple. Over six years, more than 60,000 hectares (150,000 acres) of scrubland would be cultivated. Local labour would be used to plant the peanuts and machines would harvest them. The oil would be sent back to Britain. So far, so good. On paper the scheme made perfect sense. On land, the reality was very different.

In April 1946 the Overseas Food Corporation sent a team of civil servants to Tanganyika. They were led by a former Director of Agriculture called John Wakefield. Their mission was to find suitable sites for cultivation. They reported that the land was suitable for such a scheme. They also said that modern farming equipment would make the process straightforward.

The Groundnut Army

The project team began to advertise for local labourers to work for the "Groundnut Army" and over 100,000 people came forward. The first area to be cleared was in central Tanganyika at a place called Kongwa. Peanuts had already been grown there. Everyone involved was very optimistic that the scheme would be a resounding success.

Tractor traumas

The first job was to clear the land of large baobab trees, native bushes, grasses, and bamboo. The problem was that there weren't any tractors or bulldozers available. The team tried recycling old tanks and transforming them into agricultural machinery but met with little success. Eventually some tractors were ordered from Canada and the Philippines. Once the tractors got to the main port of Dar-es-Salaam, they had to be transported to Kongwa, 350 kilometres (220 miles) away, by a single-track steam railway.

Then, just as things seemed to be moving, a **flash flood** wiped out the railway line and the tractors had to be transported on a dirt road. By February 1947, only 16 small tractors had arrived in Kongwa. Perhaps the project team should have read the signs and given up there and then.

When the task of clearing the land finally began, the tractors weren't up to the task. Baobab trees can be 18 metres (59 feet) tall and 9 metres (30 feet) round. Digging them up was nearly impossible. Within a few short months, most of the imported tractors had been wrecked.

The dry village

Tanganyika was a hot country with a dusty, dry climate. John Wakefield and his team had to build a village to house the workers, store equipment, and hopefully, store peanuts too. Oddly, they decided to build it away from a water source. Water had to be transported in and stored in a concrete pool.

Tractors like this one were used to clear land for the peanut crops. They often broke down.

Washed and baked

The "Groundnut Army" finally planted the first nuts in the autumn of 1947. However, this wasn't the end of the problems. The rainy season came and flash floods washed away some of the storage buildings in the village. The following spring the sun baked the ground so hard the workers struggled to harvest the nuts.

The original target of clearing and planting 60,000 hectares (150,000 acres) was reduced to 20,000 hectares (50,000 acres). After two years, only 2,000 tonnes (2,205 tons) of peanuts had been harvested. The Tanganyika Groundnut Scheme was finally declared a failure and cancelled in 1951.

What was learned?

The British project team assumed that the local African farmers used inferior techniques. They didn't consult them or use their knowledge. As a result, virtually every choice made regarding soil, machines, labour, and land was wrong. By the time it admitted failure, the British government had spent nearly £50 million. As with species introductions, it is vital to fully understand the environment and the impact we can have on it. Imposing a scheme without real knowledge led to disaster in Tanganyika and left the people there jobless and with **barren** land.

The combine harvesters were so inefficient that almost half the peanut crop had to be picked by hand.

The Dustbowl

Nearly 80 years ago, another environmental disaster partly caused by humans led to a new term – the Dustbowl. Just as they did in Tanganyika, humans had underestimated the negative impact they could have on the land.

The Great Plains of America are flat, fertile, and cover an area of approximately 2.9 million square kilometres (1.1 million square miles) from Texas to Canada. In the early 1930s a severe drought in the region made the land so dry that it cracked open. Decades of intensive farming had left the topsoil loose and powdery. Wild grasses had been removed by ploughing. When the winds came, there was nothing to hold the soil to the ground.

After the experience of the Dustbowl, lessons were learned and farming methods in America changed. Soil protection became a priority. Today **crop rotation** allows the land to recover by ensuring that the same crop is not planted on a piece of land year after year.

Black blizzards

Throughout the 1930s a series of freak storms hit the Great Plains. Hundreds of thousands of tonnes of topsoil were blown off and up into gigantic dust clouds. Whole towns were buried in dust during what became known as "black blizzards". Day after day the storms hit the land. People lost their homes, crops were ruined, and livestock was blinded or killed by the dust.

In 1937, residents of the town of Springfield in Colorado, USA watched as a dust cloud approached. They were plunged into darkness when the "black blizzard" finally reached them.

The Great Sparrow Campaign

Mao Zedong was the leader of China from 1949 until his death in 1976. He had total power and used a vast army to control the Chinese people. Mao wanted to increase harvests in China to reduce the chance of famine and so that the country could **export** more agricultural produce. This plan, he believed, would benefit the whole country.

Mao declared that there were "four pests" – rats, flies, mosquitoes, and sparrows. These pests were believed to be responsible for poor harvests, so between 1958 and 1962 Mao organized a mass campaign to **exterminate** sparrows. He called it "our battle of destruction". Many scientists tried to tell Mao that he was making a mistake but he wouldn't take their advice.

Famine was widespread in China in the 1940s and 1950s. These people from Hunan Province are begging for food in 1946.

The Great Leap Forward

Mao had a plan called the Great Leap Forward that he thought would make China the most efficient farming country on Earth. He believed that Chinese agriculture could be transformed by organizing millions of peasant farmers into groups known as collectives.

The Great Sparrow Campaign was part of the Great Leap Forward and was just one of the reasons that Mao's Great Leap didn't go forwards. Instead it went tragically backwards.

Pots and pans

Chinese peasants were told to rush out into the fields, bang on pots and pans, and scream at the top of their voices. They did as Mao ordered because nobody dared to disobey. Even children went out and shouted at the birds. All the commotion made the sparrows eating the seeds take flight. They stayed in the air as long as they could before they became exhausted and fell to the ground, where they died.

All over China, nests were torn down, eggs broken, and sparrow chicks killed. Prizes and rewards were offered to whoever killed the most sparrows. The people were locked in a deadly fight to exterminate the "pests".

In 1958 and 1959 the Great Sparrow Campaign appeared to be working. Increased crop **yield** was recorded. Mao was keen to appear as a miracle worker to the outside world. He put pressure on his officials to report good harvests even when the truth was quite different.

Vital links in the chain

Sparrows, like all animals, have an important place in the **food chain**. Food chains need balance to stay under control. As well as eating seeds and worms, sparrows feed on locusts. With no sparrows to eat them, locust populations grew so much that they swarmed. Farms across China were hit by plagues of locusts that destroyed crops.

Poor harvests led to a famine that killed 38 million people. That's more than half the population of the United Kingdom. The situation was desperate. Whole regions of farm labourers were wiped out. Yet Mao's officials kept giving him the numbers he wanted to see. The country was apparently enjoying record harvests. From 1958 to 1960 China continued to export grain to other countries, while its own people were starving.

Change of plan

In 1960 Mao finally started to listen to his scientific advisers and ordered the end of the Great Sparrow Campaign. Even so, people were so stirred up by the government's rewards for killing sparrows that it was at least another year before the large-scale killing of sparrows stopped.

Scientists don't always agree and they sometimes get things wrong. Usually though, they get things right and so it's important not to ignore the evidence. Interfering so dramatically with the food chain is something that we've now learned has unexpected consequences. Mao's "pest programme" did eliminate sparrows from Chinese farms and it did work to start with. However, the natural food chain was disrupted. The swarming locusts destroyed the very crops that were intended to prevent famine.

Many of the ways in which farmers have dealt with pests can be harmful to people, animals, and the environment. This picture, taken in 1955, shows some of the different fertilizers and pesticides used then, including DDT, which was later found to be a cause of cancer (see page 14).

The new "Four Pests"

In 2004 the Chinese authorities announced a new pest campaign. People were urged to wipe out cockroaches, rats, and badgers instead of sparrows. Posters were put up in cities but not as many people responded to the campaign this time.

An imposter

Hiding away in the sugar cane fields of Queensland, Australia lurks an imposter. It is a creature so poisonous that it has been known to kill crocodiles. Meet the cane toad.

In the 1930s Australian farmers were worried about the native grey-back cane beetles that were ruining their valuable sugar cane crops. The cane toad had already been successfully introduced to eat beetles in the cane fields of Hawaii and the Philippines, so Australian farmers imported some and released them into their own fields.

An unbalanced ecology

Rather than eat the cane beetles, the toads enjoyed an easy alternative diet in the form of native lizards, frogs, mice, and even small snakes. As a result, the cane toad is responsible for dwindling numbers of native reptiles while the cane beetle continued to eat the sugar cane!

Pest controller turned pest

The cane toad's skin and even its tadpoles are highly **toxic** to other animals if eaten. With no natural **predators**, the number of cane toads has grown and they have become a form of pest. Scientists now think they may have found a natural, native answer to stop the cane toad's dominance. The meat ant is a native Australian species that is known to consume anything – even poisonous cane toads.

This cane toad has made the trip from sugar cane fields to a garden in the suburbs of Queensland, Australia.

Biofuels and the great greenwash

The world is running out of oil. This important resource is used to fuel our transport and to make textiles, plastics, and medicine. Concerns about lack of oil and climate change caused by burning oil mean that alternative fuels need to be found.

Plant power?

Some people think the answer to our fuel problems may be found in plants. Scientists all over the world have been researching biofuels. Biofuels are made in different ways. One way is to harvest plants and **ferment** them to produce the fuel ethanol. Crops such as corn, sugar beet, sugar cane, or palm can be used for this. Another way is to treat cooking oil and use it to fuel diesel-powered vehicles.

Biofuels are seen as different to **fossil fuels** even though both types of fuel give off harmful carbon emissions when they are burned. Biofuels are made from plants, which means they are a **renewable** source of energy. Unlike fossil fuels, they won't run out.

An old idea

Some of the very first cars were fuelled by plants. For example, in 1900 Rudolf Diesel introduced a car that ran on peanut oil. Later cars used petrol because it was cheaper and more efficient.

Here, Henry Ford is at the wheel of his Model T car, which ran on the biofuel ethanol.

The cost to the environment

Biofuels have many potential problems. For example, the crops to make the fuel take up an enormous amount of land. Millions of hectares would need to be used if biofuels were to replace oil. There is already a shortage of farmland, so more rainforests would have to be cut down.

Another problem is that producing biofuels creates large amounts of carbon dioxide, which contributes to climate change. Fertilizers, as well as the fuel used to power tractors and other farm machinery, produce carbon dioxide.

Indonesia is made up of a group of islands in South East Asia.

Indonesia is one of the world's largest producers of biofuel. Its tropical climate is perfect for harvesting palm oil. Palm oil is used in snack foods, soaps, and cosmetics as well as being used to fuel vehicles. Indonesia is an economically developing country and the government sees palm oil as a valuable part of the economy. The problem is that farmers are cutting down and clearing rainforest in order to increase their plantations.

Slash and burn

Approximately 50 per cent of Indonesia is covered with rainforest. Less than fifty years ago, over 80 per cent was forest. As the forests are cleared, plantations, including those used to produce palm oil, are established. Between 1985 and 2009 the land used for palm oil plantations increased from 600,000 hectares (1.5 million acres) to nearly 10 million hectares (25 million acres).

When rainforest is cut down, it's not just the trees that vanish. Deforestation in Indonesia is responsible for the near extinction of animals such as the orangutan and Sumatran tiger. It is estimated that over 50 per cent of the world's plant species live in rainforests. Many of our medicines have come from rainforest plants and if the forests are cut down, the chances of finding cures for serious diseases are reduced. Most importantly of all, forests absorb carbon dioxide, the main greenhouse gas that leads to global warming. If we cut the forests down, the planet will get warmer more quickly.

These palm oil seedlings have been planted on fallow land (land that has been cleared but not used for a time). By using fallow land instead of clearing new areas of rainforest, some farmers in Indonesia are helping to save the forests as well as the animals that live in them.

41

Environment or economy?

Environmentalists know that cutting down rainforest to plant biofuel crops is ecologically counterproductive. Rainforests are "carbon sinks". This means that billions of tonnes of carbon are absorbed by the trees, plants, and soil of the forest. When the forests are burned and cleared, all the carbon stored there gets released into the atmosphere and increases global warming, the very thing that the use of biofuels is trying to avoid.

The problem is that Indonesia is an economically developing country. The people there need jobs and money, so forests are cut down and the wider environmental impact is ignored. Strong regulation is needed if the forest clearances are to stop.

Future fantastic?

India is one of the world's largest economies and it is developing fast. The Indian government wants to be energy self-sufficient within five years and is producing its own biofuel crop. The pretty jatropha plant has oil-rich seeds and it is being harvested across the country but not on cleared forest land. Jatropha oil is even cheaper than palm oil at around US$43 per barrel and its **yield** per hectare is the same. In the future it could become the world's most important plant.

Greenwashing

Buying groceries can be confusing. It seems every product is trying to "outgreen" the next with eco-friendly claims. In 2009 a study of American supermarket items found that 98 per cent of "eco-friendly" products made false or misleading claims on the packaging. This is called "greenwashing", a method of covering up the negative elements of a product and focusing on the good bits. It's the same with biofuels. The fuel is green but clearing forests isn't.

The oil from these jatropha plants is used to fuel trains on the Mumbai to Delhi railway line.

Jet Jatropha

The airline industry has been a heavy user of oil. However, lessons have been learned and the future may be more positive. On 30 December 2008, Air New Zealand successfully completed a test flight from Auckland using a fuel mixture of jatropha oil and jet fuel.

What has been learned?

As we have seen, biofuels come with their own problems. They can be just as bad for the environment as fossil fuels. They also risk creating food shortages, as more and more plant crops are sold to biofuel manufacturers. We are still learning and making mistakes in the search for an environmentally safe fuel.

The greatest challenge for scientists and leaders all around the world today is efficient energy creation. Oil is running out and there is an urgent need to reduce carbon emissions. Governments and scientists need to find an energy source that is clean and green.

Nuclear power can provide energy quickly and produces virtually no air pollution, unlike **fossil fuels**. Burning oil, gas, and coal generates massive amounts of carbon dioxide and leads to global warming. However, it's not easy to control nuclear power. It also produces dangerous waste that must be disposed of safely.

Design fault

Early nuclear plants weren't designed to contain radiation or to limit leaks when meltdowns occurred (see panel). The Santa Susana Field Laboratory was an early nuclear reactor test facility near Los Angeles, USA. In 1959 the laboratory suffered a partial meltdown but there were no concrete containment structures to hold the radiation. As a result, **radioactive** gases were released into the atmosphere. Many of the laboratory workers died of cancer caused by the radiation. Scientific knowledge of the problems involved in controlling nuclear reactions has improved a lot since the Santa Susana accident and lessons were learned, but it wasn't until the Chernobyl disaster nearly thirty years later that the world really started to take notice of the containment issue.

Fizzing fission

Nuclear power is produced when small, carefully controlled nuclear explosions are created. This is done using **atoms** from the radioactive chemical elements uranium or plutonium. When atoms of nuclear fuel split, they produce heat. This is called fission. The energy produced by fission is used to heat water that is turned into steam. This then drives a turbine to make electricity. The radioactive chemicals are used in the form of solid fuel rods that need to be cooled constantly. If the reactions speed out of control, too much heat is created. Explosions can happen and **toxic** radiation can leak out. This is called meltdown.

Timebomb

It was early on a Sunday morning on 26 April 1986 at the Chernobyl nuclear power plant in northern Ukraine. Scientists were testing the nuclear reactor to see how long the turbines could produce energy in the event of a loss of power. The reactor's cooling system was turned off and the reactor was run at low power. This was despite the fact that scientists knew the reactor was unstable at low power settings.

FAIL!

The force of the explosion at the Chernobyl nuclear power plant destroyed the reactor building.

Countdown to disaster

With the cooling system off, the Chernobyl reactor became unstable. To counter this, operators removed over twenty **control rods,** leaving only six or eight to maintain the system's delicate balance. Safety procedures at the plant stated that the reactor should be shut down if there weren't enough control rods to keep the reactor safe in the event of a power surge. The scientists wanted to finish their test so they ignored the rules.

Steam and pressure built up to over 100 times the normal rate and the fuel overheated. The control rods couldn't be re-inserted in time to cool the system and at 1.23 a.m. a huge explosion rocked the plant and blew a hole in the reactor dome. Several more explosions followed.

People in the nearby town of Pripyat were woken by the blast and rushed to their windows to see a big cloud appear across the moon. All through the rest of the night and into the coming days, a super-fine, barely visible dust gently fell down over the town, on to the land, into the rivers, and into the air.

This map shows you where Chernobyl is.

Secret explosion

At the time of the explosion, Ukraine was part of the secretive **USSR** and so details of exactly what had happened and how serious the accident was took weeks to filter out. It was two days after the explosion that scientists in Sweden first detected a high level of radioactive dust particles in the air. Tracing the wind direction back, they realized that something serious must have happened.

Managing meltdown

People all over the world had feared that this kind of accident could happen – a nuclear accident that could have **catastrophic** effects on the environment. The environmental impact of Chernobyl is massive. There is a 30 kilometre (20 mile) Zone of Alienation around the reactor where nobody is allowed to go because it is still so radioactive. Scientists estimate it will be 20,000 years before this area will be safe for any human or agricultural activity. Scientists disagree on the overall impact but most accept that at least 4,000 people have died so far as a direct result of being exposed to radiation after the accident.

The Chernobyl disaster showed how much scientists still had to learn about safely controlling nuclear reactors and power station design. One lesson learned, though, is the importance of establishing and following safety procedures.

A high-ranking disaster

The Chernobyl accident is the worst nuclear power plant disaster in history. The International Nuclear Event Scale measured the explosion as a level 7, the highest rank. This means an event that has caused widespread environmental and health effects.

Safety first

Today reinforced (strengthened) concrete and steel cases are built around nuclear reactors as a safety measure. The poorly planned Chernobyl reactor had no such containment structure. If anything goes wrong with the fission process, radiation should be contained within the concrete structure where it cannot endanger people or the environment. Construction of all nuclear power plants is monitored by the International Atomic Energy Agency to ensure that safety comes first. We have learned a lot about reactor containment, but there's one more key lesson to learn – what to do with the waste.

Waste management

A large nuclear reactor produces 3 cubic metres (105 cubic feet) of waste fuel each year. There are over 400 nuclear power plants worldwide.

Mafia madness

Governments pay big money to specialist companies to dispose of nuclear waste properly. In Italy the **Mafia** has got involved in this **lucrative** industry. In 2009, drums of nuclear waste were discovered washed up on Mediterranean beaches. An **informant** said that instead of disposing of the waste safely, the Mafia ordered ships that were carrying waste to be blown up at sea.

These containers of low-level nuclear waste are being responsibly disposed of in a safe location at Hanford in Washington, USA.

That makes a lot of radioactive waste to dispose of every year. The most effective storage system currently available is to bury waste in steel and concrete containers. However, no one has the perfect solution yet, and the amount of waste is increasing all the time. By 2007 the United States alone had 50,000 tonnes (55,000 tons) of radioactive waste. A solution needs to be found, and soon.

Designing the future

We have already learned many things about safety but the issues of safe nuclear energy production, containment, and waste disposal remain huge environmental challenges at the start of the 21st century. With coal-fired power stations contributing to global warming, alternative energy sources need to be found and governments all over the world are looking at nuclear power as the answer.

Scientists have now begun work on the next generation of nuclear power stations that may solve some of those problems. Still at a theoretical stage, researchers think they can construct a process that recycles old nuclear waste in the production of electricity. The waste that would be produced in the new power plants would only remain radioactive for a few decades rather than thousands of years.

What has been learned?

Our nuclear know-how is increasing all the time. We have learned how to design better power stations and we now appreciate the scale of the waste problem. In time we may come to control and contain this power fully. The French politician Christian Bataille has said, "Today we stock containers of waste because currently scientists don't know how to reduce or eliminate the **toxicity**, but maybe in 100 years perhaps scientists will..." If we learn our lessons well, he might just be right.

Some major invasive species

All over the world, invasive species such as kudzu and Nile perch are a problem. Sometimes humans are at fault, while at other times the power of nature just takes over. The species listed here are taken from the Global Invasive Species Group's top 100 of the world's worst.

Pushy possum

The common brushtail possum was introduced to New Zealand by European settlers in the 19th century in an attempt to establish a fur industry. They soon escaped into the wild, where they have thrived as an invasive species. In 2009 there were estimated to be around 70 million possums. There are no native **predators** of the possum in New Zealand. There have been many attempts to get rid of them because of the damage they do to native trees and wildlife. They are also carriers of disease.

Far-reaching fern

The Giant Salvinia fern (*Salvinia molesta*) is native to Brazil. It grows rapidly and floats on water, forming dense mats that make it difficult for boats to sail through it. It also clogs drains, chokes fish, and smothers other plants. It has become an invasive species in many countries, such as Australia, New Zealand, Sri Lanka, India, and the United States. Giant Salvinia was first seen in the United States in a South Carolina pond in 1995. By 2004 the United States Geological Society reported that the fern had spread to water systems in more than 11 states.

Clam attack!

In the San Francisco Bay area of California, Chinese clams have caused a major ecological imbalance. The clams can grow as densely as 10,000 per square metre (10 square feet) and large populations have established themselves in the waters of the bay. Their feeding habits are affecting native fish species. The clams filter plankton out of the water leaving very little behind for the fish species who also depend on it for food.

Suffocating seaweed

The seaweed *Caulerpa taxifolia* is a particularly nasty invasive species. So far it has contaminated 13,000 hectares (32,000 acres) of the Mediterranean Sea and similar areas off the Californian and Australian coastlines. It doesn't actually kill, but it stifles other marine **ecosystems** by forming dense carpets. Measures aimed at combating it by introducing seaweed-loving tropical snails haven't worked yet.

Rats running wild

The common European rat has spread to most parts of the world by sneaking on to boats. Since sailors first started exploring, rats have been stowing away and setting foot on new land at the same time as humans. In places such as New Zealand and Hawaii, where many of the native birds are flightless, rats often eat eggs and young chicks. This has pushed many bird species to the point of extinction.

Glossary

archipelago group or chain of islands

atom smallest part of a chemical element

barren infertile

bioaccumulation process by which a substance builds up inside the bodies of living things

brainchild original idea

cash crop crop grown to sell rather than consume

catastrophe total disaster

colonial rule ruling over another country

conscience sense of right and wrong

control rods rods made out of the mineral graphite. They are inserted into the core of a nuclear reactor to control the speed at which atoms will split and produce energy.

crop rotation when a crop that is different from the previous year's crop is planted in the same area

desalination removal of salt

disperse spread out

distil purify through boiling

dredge dig underwater

dugong large plant-eating sea mammal

ecosystem organisms interacting in balance with their environment and each other

export send goods or produce abroad

exterminate completely destroy

ferment break down a substance using bacteria or yeast

flash flood sudden and often destructive surge of water

food chain series of organisms, each of which is dependent on the next as a source of food

fossil fuel fuel derived from decomposed plant and animal remains, such as coal, peat, oil, or gas

geothermal describing heat from Earth's interior

gondola canal boat used in Venice

hybrid plant or animal produced from cross-breeding

impenetrable dense, impassable

informant someone who gives confidential information to the police

insecticide chemical substance used to kill insects

irrigation bringing water to a dry area

lucrative very profitable

Mafia secret criminal organization originating in Sicily

malnourished having a poor diet

predator animal that feeds on other animals

radioactive decaying plutonium or uranium that can be harmful to humans exposed to it

renewable source of energy produced from natural resources, such as the sun, wind, and plants

sediment settled sand and rock at the bottom of the sea

toxic highly poisonous

toxicity amount of poison in a substance or material

USSR Union of Soviet Socialist Republics (also known as the Soviet Union). The communist state that existed from 1922 to 1991, including Russia and 14 other republics.

yield amount produced, harvest

Find out more

Books

Alien Invasion: Invasive Species Become Major Menaces,
   Cari Jackson (Gareth Stevens Publishing, 2009)

Earth Matters: Made With Care (Dorling Kindersley, 2008)

Fossil Fuels and Biofuels, Elizabeth Raum
   (Heinemann Library, 2008)

*Rachel Carson: Fighting Pesticides and Other Chemical
   Pollutants*, Patricia Lantier (Crabtree Publishing, 2009)

Science Missions: Building the Three Gorges Dam, Patricia Kite
      (Raintree, 2010)

Websites

www.recyclezone.org.uk
You can learn how to reduce, reuse, and recycle on this website.

**www.nhm.ac.uk/nature-online/environmental-change/
index.html**
The Natural History Museum website has lots of information
about climate change, as well as some tips about how you can
help fight it.

http://environment.nationalgeographic.co.uk/environment
You can find information about environmental projects and
disasters on this website.

Further research

Artificial islands:

- Look up Federation Island in the Black Sea, where the 2014 Winter Olympics will be held.
- Four artificial islands are being built off the coast of Israel to take the pressure off crowded cities. What will happen to the sea life?

Deforestation:

- Logging projects in US national parks
- Oil exploration in the Alaskan wilderness

Nuclear accidents:

- Three Mile Island, USA. This accident happened in 1979 and is the United States' worst civilian nuclear disaster.

Construction projects:

- Three Gorges Dam, China. This dam holds back the Yangtze, one of the largest rivers on Earth.

Tourism:

- Galapagós Islands. How are large numbers of visitors affecting this fragile ecosystem?
- Look up protected places on the United Nations' World Heritage List.

Science:

- Research the environmental experiment called Biosphere-2 – a large, sealed greenhouse that aims to recreate natural environments. Find out what happened when seven scientists went to live there.

Index